No Trace Left:
Internet Privacy Tips and Strategies to Protect Your Personal and Financial Information

By: R.J. Simmons

Disclaimer

Published by:
R.J. Simmons and Random Technologies
4409 HOFFNER AVENUE, SUITE 347
Belle Isle, FL 32812

Table of Contents

Table of Contents

Introduction

Thank you! Your purchase means a lot to me, and I hope that this book meets your expectations.

Technology does a lot of great things for society. It helps us make medical advances, pay bills easier, and even connect with each other across long distances. These things are all admirable, but they do not come without a cost.

Today's technology poses a huge threat to your privacy, financial and personal. Unfortunately the federal government has stepped over the line of protecting its people, and into the realm of monitoring its people. The CIA, the FBI, and even the military have all been used to gather information on United States citizens (aka 'suspected terrorists' 'anti-war protestors' and 'communists').

This isn't new, but it is stronger than ever. The American government collects ridiculous amount of information on each of its citizens, all in the name of protecting the State, for its own personal gains.

If you're looking for evidence of this, just look at what Google searches can tell you. A Google search for a person often yields enough information for the identity of the searchee to be successfully stolen.

Identity thieves only compound this danger by sending emails, skimming ATMs, and operating ID scams that only serve to worsen the risks to your privacy.

What's the worst that could happen? Ask a victim of identity theft, who has just found out their bank account, is now empty, or their credit cards are maxed out – or maybe even that they have new credit cards and car payments they never signed up for. Taking your life back after your identity has been stolen can take months to years, the whole time more damage is being done to you.

These are just the malicious risks on the part of identity theft villains, and say nothing of the risks of the government having access to all of this information on you at any given moments notice.

So what can you do? This guide will outline simple things you can do to ensure the safety of you and your family's personal information. This guide will emphasize the cheapest and best ways to change your risk level from high to not at all.

By making it more difficult for people to access your information, it doesn't mean no one will access it, but it does mean that a lot of other people will look like easier targets – and that only experts will really know how to get to who 'you' are.

Our privacy is constantly under attack and for all of my readers, I give you complimentary updates to the latest threats to your personal and financial privacy – with solutions and steps to take to protect your information.

**STAY connected by Subscribing to Our FREE Newsletter:
www.NoTraceLeft.com**

Ready? Let's look at some solutions.

Online Privacy

Don't use email service from Hotmail to Yahoo and Gmail, there are a lot of web hosting services that offer free email services for interested users.

People use these emails for professional communication, personal communication, and checking messages from afar on their mobile phones. It's the key to staying connected throughout the day.

The danger comes in with using a free email service, but especially when using Yahoo.

So what makes Yahoo so dangerous? Since 2013, thousands of Yahoo users have been hacked. This hacking is malicious and it often allows for hackers to send out virus ridden unknown links to your contact list.

The problem is exacerbated by the fact that many Yahoo users report not clicking any unknown links or opening a malicious message – pointing to hacking vulnerabilities through no fault of the users.

Yahoo claims its working to address these issues, but so far the results seem to say otherwise. This is negligence, and it is just one of the many reasons you shouldn't use Yahoo as your free email client of choice.

Hide Your IP

An IP address is your computer's online identifier, and links to your location as well. It is assigned by your ISP (internet service provider), and provides hackers with access to your location. This enables skilled hackers to track down exactly where you're writing from with minimal effort.

On top of hackers being able to see you, the government can trace your location when you post on blogs, send emails, or even post statuses. The American government has indeed become quite concerned with the 'free' speech of its citizens, and using your real name and not masking your IP address only makes this process easier.

What can you do? Protect yourself by hiding your IP address, consider using a VPN – virtual private network. A virtual private network re-routes your computer's connection to the internet around the world, making it a lot more difficult for someone to trace where you actually are.

VPNs also have the added benefits of removing area restrictions on the internet. This has different meanings depending on where you're located in the world. If you're travelling to Canada, it means you can still watch Hulu.com videos whenever you want. If you're off in China, you can still get unrestricted access to news.

A recommended VPN service is Hotspot Shield, found at www.hotspotshield.com/en. There are trials available.

Make Your Password SECURE!

Christopher Chaney took a year long period (from 2010-2011) to prove the dangers of poor passwords. How did he do it? He hacked celebrity email accounts, retrieved embarrassingly personal information, and posted it online.

You might be thinking Mr. Chaney must be a gifted hacker, but in reality he simply used publicly available data to figure out the security questions, got into an email account, and used their contact list to find other email addresses to hack.

The problem that's underlying here is that these passwords were very clearly based on easy to figure out personal information. Yours shouldn't be. Consider the following tips when working up to creating your password.

Password creation tips:
- Change your password at least once every three months
- Use letters, numbers, symbols, and punctuation marks if possible
- Make your password longer than eight characters
- Use different passwords for different accounts
- Do not use common themes: your family member's name, words spelled backwards

These may seem like logical, easy to follow tips, but they can take some effort to get used to. However, if you do, you will be well on your way to increasing your security.

Check this free website and test the strength of your passwords: https://howsecureismypassword.net

Make Your Chat Life Private

Message boards, forums, chat rooms. Three great ways to connect with other human beings. And to be found by anyone who is looking for what your opinions are or ways to secretly put you on the record.

So what can you do? Consider using a program like Cryptocat that allows users to go online and communicate like normal, but with the additional option of setting up private chatrooms that automatically dispose after exited.

In addition, this chatroom is encryptable. Only you and the person you've provided the password to can enter the chat, and only you two can see the conversation.

You can download Cryptocat from https://crypto.cat – and it's free to use.

A Quick Install That Keeps You Covered

It's become common practice for all websites to track their users activity. From tracking your location, to collecting information about which ads you've clicked on, the sites you visit are doing their best to sell forms of your identity for profit.

But they aren't the bad guys. Identity thieves, hackers, and even the government are people you should be more worried about having access to your information.

Consider using Tor. First developed by the American Navy, Tor is a program that hides your tracks as you go throughout the internet by encrypting data and re-routing it through different areas so that people can't figure out what exactly you've been clicking or where you're clicking from. In fact, Tor even anonymizes the amount of clicks and data that have been made by you.

"Tor is a network of virtual tunnels." These are the words of the developers, and they are used to describe the shroud of secrecy that people are in when they use Tor to hide their online tracks.

Whether a journalist, a whistleblower, a social critic, or even just an individual, consider using Tor. One of the best parts about Tor? It's free. Go to https://www.torproject.org/ to get your hands on this great software that can help secure your connection safety.

Encrypt Your Emails

Even beyond avoiding using the wrong kinds of free email hosts, you can encrypt your emails with freeware. This means that readers and writers will need to enter a password to gain access to the emails you're sending.

Pretty Good Privacy (PGP) is open source and offers a degree of protection for both your emails and your files that the government itself struggles to break. Both sender and receiver require a password, and they are not breakable passwords.

There are a lot of different versions of PGP, including GnuPG at https://www.gnupg.org/.

Keeping Safe, Even In Public

Ever heard the cautions about being careful about logging onto public Wi-Fi? It's true, you should be paying attention. Because although the coffee shop is providing you with free internet access to get you in the door, there are other people around who often wait to gain access to personal information.

What can you do about it? Change settings on your computers file explorer and browser. In terms of which ones in particular you should be worried about, wonder about 'sharing' settings and network discovery.

Sharing settings allow file sharing, which can be great if you're trying to get your boyfriend to listen to that song – but not so great if you're trying to stay safe when logging on in public.

Here's how to alter your sharing settings:

On Windows – 5 steps -

Step 1) Click start, scroll over settings, and click control panel

Step 2) Click network and sharing center

Step 3) Go to the area where you can alter your homegroup and sharing options.

Step 4) Go to advanced sharing settings

Step 5) Turn off file sharing and public folder sharing

On Macs

Step 1) Go to system preferences

Step 2) Go to sharing

Step 3) Deselect all sharing preferences

Here's how to alter your network discovery settings:

On Windows

Step 1) Still in advanced sharing settings, uncheck the network discovery settings

On Macs

Step 1) Go to system preferences

Step 2) Go to security

Step 3) Go to firewall

Step 4) Go into stealth mode by clicking the box

Use HTTPS Feature EVERYWHERE

Have you ever looked at the link you're using and noticed that instead of beginning with 'http://' it begins with 'https://'? The s in this sequence actually stands for security, as in increased security indulged in by the website you're currently visiting.

This indulgence means that any communication between the server and the user is directly private and that you are on the site your computer is claiming you're on. This prevents people from interrupting your computer's connection with a server and getting involved with your online banking or email.

The issue we have is that you should be using https functions ALL the time, not just when websites decide to offer it to you. Https Everywhere is a Chrome/Firefox extension that allows just that, its users to always be on https secure webpages for over 3,000 popular webpages.

You can get the extension here: https://www.eff.org/https-everywhere and can use it on thousands of webpages.

Avoid Free Applications

Androids and iPhones have done a great job of making apps the first step in getting a new phone. From Angry Birds to Free Calendar, the smartphone era is designed to add piles of functionality to your phone. But it also compromises your security if you're not careful.

Ever read those user agreements? Most of them (60% of iPhone apps, 42% of Android apps) have you agree to share your contacts information, your calendar information, and your location, to help target advertisements towards you.

A lot of people don't necessarily see the danger of this, but the danger is real, and it's more in what lays beneath the targeting – the idea that advertisers are tracking you.

How do you avoid this? Buy your apps. It may seem like a high price, but it allows you to avoid any security compromising.

Offline Security

Stay off of drones' radar

Drones, or unmanned remote controlled aerial vehicles, have been around for years now. Developed by the military, they are often used for surveillance and assassination purposes.

The problem is that drone strikes have become an all too regular occurrence. It seems like it's almost to the point that every time you turn on the news you can hear about another drone strike in the Middle East.

In fact, since President Barrack Obama has taken office, 400 drone strikes have been ordered – and not all drone activity has been restricted to the Middle East. In 2011, there were 295 active drones have been spotted flying over American soil on a regular basis, according to the Federal Aviation Administration. This means that drones seem to be fulfilling some purpose on American soil.

The drones have yet to be considered 'armed and dangerous', but the fact that they're here should be concerning enough. The other alarming fact about the drones is their developers, who have successfully armed American police with drones with Tasers, tear gas, and rubber bullets – it's not unforeseeable that these supplies will be getting used some time.

If that doesn't already have you thinking, consider the statements made by US Attorney General Eric Holder, who is on the Congress record as having said that it was "unlikely but possible" that drones would be needed to defend American soil, and that targeting American citizens cannot be ruled out.

I'm not saying drones are necessarily outside your window right now, but I am saying they could be a lot closer than you thought and that this may warrant some form of preparation.

So what can you do? Consider investing in anti-drone materials that make it harder for you to be seen by drones. Adam Harvey, an American artist from New York, offers a line of anti-drone clothing here: www.primitivelondon.co.uk

Learn How to Find a "Skimmer" Before You Get Scammed

Skimmers are devices that help scam artists record your credit card number and often gain access to your pin. In terms of how this is done, a skimmer is attached to the device in question (one where you would place a card, like an ATM), and a camera is often placed within line of sight for where you would enter your pin number.

Skimmers are primarily used at gas pumps and ATMs, but have also been found on parking meters, ticket kiosks, and pretty much any other place where money changes hands electronically.

So how do you spot skimmers?

- Pay attention any time ANY ONE asks to hold your card. Skimmers can be used quickly, and your card only needs to be out of your eyesight for a second for the crime to occur.
- Pay attention to your surroundings, and block the pinpad with your hands, to prevent your pin being stolen.
- Wherever possible, use ATMs inside of banks or respectable places of business only, as these are harder targets for skimmers.
- Pay attention to the condition of the place where you are about to slide your card – is it cracked, damaged, etc.
- Avoid public ATMs whenever possible, particularly ones that are available for public use (as these are popular targets for skimmer scammers)

These tips don't guarantee your safety from skimming scams, but they do go a long way towards helping you become less likely to become a victim. The final tip we have is that you check your credit card statements regularly for irregular activity, in case you have been the victim of a skimming scam.

Keep Your Passport Safe

Since 2007, all passports have had Radio Frequency Identification Tags (RFID) embedded in them by the government. (These RFID chips are also stored in licenses in Michigan, New York, Vermont, and Washington). This chip stores your information: your birthday, your gender, your nationality, your birth place, and a photo. It may one day go one step further and even include fingerprint data and more, but for now this information is threatening enough.

Though developed by the government and though they are said to be 'secure', RFID tags are easily read by identity thieves. All they need to do is cruise around town, finding people carrying their passports, with a machine in their pocket that grabs the Homeland security file number, and these cards will naturally be cloned.

There is a small form of security in that the information itself is still inaccessible so far even with this file number, but hackers are not far from gaining access to it – and thus to thousands of identities to steal and ruin.

So what can you do? Work to keep your RFID tags safe, by always keeping any documents containing RFID chips in aluminium or stainless steel 'shields' that block signal.

RFID shields are available for purchase on Amazon.

Keep Your Home Secure, As Affordably As Possible

When trying to keep your house secure, people try all sorts of things. From purchasing weapons for self defense to keeping alarms that try to contact emergency services for you, people spend thousands a year on home security.

One way you can affordably protect your home is by spending $10 on a two way radio that allows you to hear what's going on. Keep one near the common entry points to the house and the other with you so that you can tune in when necessary. Note, that when tuning in, you should be allowing them to hear YOU, scaring off a lot of potential burglars.

Protect Your Social Security Number

Social security numbers were created to help keep track of how much money you make and what benefits you were exactly owed. That was a very effective purpose, and it does work for that, but employers, insurance companies, and the government have since turned it into a way to identify you personally.

As a result, you need to work hard to protect your social security number. Though some people require it, for example the IRS, others have no right to it and ask for it anyway – these are people you should be refusing it to.

Whenever anyone asks for your social security number, consider the following four questions:
Question 1) Why are they asking for it?
Question 2) What will they do with it if you give it to them?
Question 3) Are you required to give it by law?
Question 4) What will happen if you don't give it?

If you can answer all of these questions, you are informed enough to decide whether or not you'd like to hand out your social security number. Just be sure to keep in mind how linked it is to your personal identity, and how easy it makes identity thieves' job when looking for a way to scam you.

Keep Your Computer Safe with Military Grade Technology

If you're like most people, your computer is your safehouse. You keep your social security number, your credit card information, and other online account information all in one place.

So what about when it gets stolen?

Laptop manufacturer Kensington did a study to investigate how often computers get stolen and found that once every minute some one's laptop is being stolen.

What can you do?
Hope that you've encrypted your files? No. That will not be enough. On top of encrypting your files, you should also be considering keeping extremely sensitive information on external hard drives.

Amazon sells encrypted external hard drives, which can provide you with the security that comes with knowing your personal information is completely secured.

Protect Your Phone Number with a Throwaway Number

Ever been asked for your phone number when you really didn't want to give it out? No, I'm not talking about at a bar, I'm talking about when a car salesman, survey consultant, or store clerk asks for your phone number and you just KNOW it's going to result in millions of telemarketing calls for you.

This often happens lately on the internet, when signing up to a new service your phone number is often required – even though you know perfectly well they have no need for it.

Being concerned about them selling it is just the beginning. Your landline phone number for instance is completely linked to your address, and your cell phone gives away your area code at the very least, if not more for a more talented information hacker.

Consider using the Hushed app for your iPhone or Android. Developed by AffinityClick (and available here: http://www.hushed.com), Hushed is an app that provides a disposable number for a given period of time.

This will help you to protect your real phone number, and still get signed up when you need to.

Protect Your Phone, Protect Your Life

People today use cell phones for everything from calendar organization to mobile banking and appointment address listing. This is all fine and dandy until their phone gets stolen or misplaced.

Much like when your computer goes missing, this can be an instant heart attack – both for your missed appointments and for your missing personal information.

So how do you protect your phone information? Simple, use three easy steps we list here:

Step 1) Devise a clever pin (not 5-4-3-2-1 or 1-2-3, a clever pin that you can remember, but thieves cannot guess). Pins are the first step to phone protection, as they deter the amateur thieves from attempting to gain access to your information.

Step 2) Use a different pin to completely lock your SIM card. SIM cards store all of your phone's information on them, and can be transferred from phone to phone – so that even if you encrypt your phone, the SIM may still give you away. Pick a pin that is different from your original phone pin, and encrypt your SIM.

Step 3) Encrypt your phone files when they are plugged into a computer. Not every one thinks of this but phone files are readily available often when the phone is attached to a computer USB drive... You can avoid making this a nightmare simply by encrypting your phone's files next time you connect.

These three steps go a long way to deterring most thieves from messing with your information, and will prevent a great deal of the risk that comes with having a stolen or missing phone.

Avoid Doing These Things on Public Computers – ALWAYS

Most people don't find themselves on public computers all too often these days. From laptops to tablets and smartphones, it's rare that a person not have instant access to their personal files – and that kind of convenience is rarely sacrificed. However, that shouldn't stop you from arming yourself with the knowledge to protect yourself and your identity when you're logging on to a public computer.

- Do not check social media accounts, bank accounts, or other personal accounts

The first reason for this is the most obvious, many people close browsers instead of logging out. This means that the next person to log on to the public computer that you used could gain access to banking information, social media networks, or even yours and your friends' addresses.

But this is the obvious danger.

The less talked about danger is the more critical one, keystroke recording software. Some skilled hackers install keystroke recorders on public computers, meaning that every single letter you type or tap of the spacebar that occurs would then be privy to prying eyes at a moments notice.

Even without keystroke software, sometimes identity thieves have been known to take up residence in public internet cafes, scanning the crowd for an unsuspecting user they can spy on.

The easiest way to protect yourself from this type of data loss, which is an aggressive type, is to simply avoid using public computers when possible; if it's not possible to avoid using a public computer, avoid checking social media or personal accounts.

Keep Your Mail Safe

A lot of effort in terms of the protection game goes into protecting your online data, or your physical person, but what about mail?

Ever thought about how often you get banking statements? Or how much of your personally identifying information is recorded on your electric bill? Identity thieves have.

They know all too well just how ignorant the average person is of the risk to themselves when they leave mail unattended. Leaving unattended mail only begs for people to comb through, steal information, and leave without you ever knowing you've been exposed to the risk.

So what can you do?

Consider the following tips to ensure your mailbox is as safe as possible:

- Do not leave mail unattended. This is a simple way to allow people to have access to your information, when you absolutely do not need to. Collect your mail regularly.

- Consider a PO Box if you have a lot of sensitive information being frequently delivered. It does cost, but it also allows your mailbox to be locked.

- Shred discarded financial documents – do not throw them out in the trash.

- Switch to online statements where possible, and again see our tips on internet information security.

Conclusions

Your privacy is at risk. The fact is it's at risk nearly all the time. Identity thieves, hackers, telemarketers, and even your government is looking to see just how much information you are willing to leave exposed – how much you're willing to put yourself at risk.

These threats are serious, and they are to our privacy, our security, and our liberty as American citizens. Every one is a target. Do not kid yourself.

If you take the steps in this guide seriously, you will be well on your way to protecting yourself from attack in every way that is possible. This is the best I can hope for you, and it's the best I can offer – and it does help.

Return to this guide whenever you need a reminder, and do your best to always protect your information like it is a part of your body.

If you found this book helpful, please share a couple of sentences and a 4-5 star review on Amazon. It would mean a great deal to me and others who are considering purchasing this book.

If you have any questions or comments, feel free to email me at rj@notraceleft.com I try to reply to all questions that come in and that I am able to.

Thank you for reading *No Trace Left: Internet Privacy Tips and Strategies to Protect Your Personal and Financial Information*

Best of luck, and be safe!
R.J. Simmons

P.S. This book is full of rich content, however I want to stay in touch. Our privacy is constantly under attack and for all of my readers, I give you complimentary updates to the latest threats to your personal and financial privacy – with solutions and steps to take to protect your information.

STAY connected by Subscribing to Our FREE Newsletter:
www.NoTraceLeft.com